THE GOSPEL OF THE FAMILY

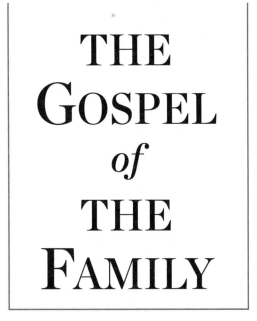

THE GOSPEL of THE FAMILY

CARDINAL WALTER KASPER

TRANSLATED BY WILLIAM MADGES

Paulist Press
New York / Mahwah, NJ

Back cover photo courtesy of the author
Cover design by Amy C. King
Book design by Lynn Else

Library of Congress Control Number: 2014935634

ISBN 978-0-8091-4908-7 (paperback)
ISBN 978-1-58768-452-4 (e-book)

Published by Paulist Press
997 Macarthur Boulevard
Mahwah, New Jersey 07430

www.paulistpress.com

Printed and bound in the
United States of America

FOREWORD

THE PRESENT SMALL VOLUME, *The Gospel of the Family,* contains the lecture that I gave under this title at the invitation of Pope Francis before the extraordinary Consistory of Cardinals on February 20 and 21, 2014, in Rome. It should provide a theological basis for the subsequent discussion among the cardinals, and introduce thereby a theologically grounded, pastoral discussion in the forthcoming synodal process at the extraordinary Synod of Bishops in fall 2014 and at the ordinary Synod of Bishops in 2015. With the consent of the pope, questions that at times have been contentiously discussed in the Church should be posed in this lecture.

The topic of the synodal process, *Pastoral Challenges to the Family in the Context of Evangelization*, makes clear that pressing pastoral questions can be handled not in isolation, but only on the basis and within the total context of the gospel and the mission of evangelization, which is common to all the baptized. For this reason, Christians who live in families and who sometimes also experience difficult family situations should not be the least of all to have a say in the discussion. This publication does not intend to preempt the response of the Synod; rather, it wants to trigger questions and prepare a foundation for them. We can arrive at a hopefully unanimous response only by walking the path of reflecting together on Jesus' message, exchanging experiences and arguments with openness, and—above all—praying together for God's Holy Spirit. May the present booklet make a modest contribution to that end.

Rome, on the feast of the apostle Matthias
February 24, 2014
Cardinal Walter Kasper

ABBREVIATIONS

AA Second Vatican Council, *Apostolicam Actuositatem:* Decree on the Apostolate of the Laity (1965).

AG Second Vatican Council, *Ad Gentes:* Decree on the Church's Missionary Activity (1965).

CCC *Catechism of the Catholic Church.* Washington: United States Catholic Conference, 1994.

DH Heinrich Denzinger, ed., *Enchiridion symbolorum: Definitionum et declarationum de rebus fidei et morum.* Freiburg: Herder, 1963.

DV Second Vatican Council, *Dei Verbum:* Dogmatic Constitution on Divine Revelation (1965).

EG Pope Francis, *Evangelii Gaudium*: Apostolic Exhortation on the Proclamation of the Gospel in Today's World (2013).

EN Pope Paul VI, *Evangelii Nuntiandi*: Apostolic Exhortation on Evangelization in Today's World (1975).

FC Pope John Paul II, *Familiaris Consortio*: Apostolic Exhortation on the Role of the Christian Family in the Modern World (1981).

GS	Second Vatican Council, *Gaudium et spes:* Pastoral Constitution on the Church in the Modern World (1965).
LG	Second Vatican Council, *Lumen Gentium:* Dogmatic Constitution on the Church (1964).
SC	Second Vatican Council, *Sacrosanctum Concilium*: Constitution on the Sacred Liturgy (1963).
UR	Second Vatican Council, *Unitatis Redintegratio*: Decree on Ecumenism (1964).

THE GOSPEL
OF THE FAMILY

INTRODUCTION:
DISCOVERING THE GOSPEL
OF THE FAMILY ANEW

In THIS INTERNATIONAL YEAR of the Family, Pope Francis has invited the Church to engage in a synodal process concerning the *Pastoral Challenges of the Family in the Context of Evangelization*. In the apostolic exhortation, *Evangelii Gaudium* [*Joy of the Gospel*], he writes, "The family is experiencing a profound cultural crisis, as are all communities and social bonds. In the case of the family, the weakening of these bonds is particularly serious because the family is the fundamental cell of society" (EG 66). Many families today see that they are confronted with serious difficulties. Many millions of people find themselves in situations of migration, flight, and forced displacement, or in degrading situations of misery, in which an orderly family life is scarcely possible. The contemporary world finds itself in an anthropological crisis. Individualism and consumerism

1

challenge the traditional culture of families. Economic conditions often make family cohesion and living together more difficult. Consequently, the number of those who back away from establishing a family or who fail to realize their life's goal, as well as the number of children who do not have the good fortune of growing up in a well-ordered family, has increased dramatically.

The church, which shares the joys and the hopes, the sorrows and the anxieties of humankind, especially the poor (GS 1), is challenged by this situation. During the last Year of the Family, Pope John Paul II modified the words of his encyclical *Redemptor Hominis* (1979), "Man is the way of the Church," and said, "The family is the way of the Church" (February 2, 1994). This is so because a human being normally comes into the world in a family and normally grows up in the bosom of a family. In all cultures in human history, the family is the normal path of human beings. Even today a large number of young people seek their life's happiness in a stable family. However, a wide gap has developed between the church's teaching concerning marriage and the family and the lived convictions of many Christians. The church's teaching appears, even to many Christians, to be out of touch with the world and with life. But we must also say and say it joyfully: there exist very good families, which do their best to live the faith of the church and give witness to the beauty and joy of faith lived in the bosom of the family. They are often a minority, but they are a distinctive minority. The current situation of the church is not unique. Even the church of the first centuries was confronted with concepts and models of marriage and family that were different from that which Jesus preached, which was quite new, both for Jews as well as for the Greeks and Romans. Therefore, our position cannot be that of a liberal accommodation to the status quo, but rather a radical position that goes back to the roots (*radices*), that is, a position that goes back to the gospel and that looks forward from that perspective. In our situation, it is, therefore, the task of the synodal process to express anew the gospel of the family, which is always the same and yet is always new (EG 1).

This lecture can neither cover the latest questions nor anticipate the outcome of the Synod, that is, the common (*syn*) path (*odos*) of the entire Church, the path of attentive listening to each other, exchanging ideas, and prayer. This lecture is intended to be a kind of overture, which introduces the topic in the hope that, at the end, we will be presented with a *sym-phony*—a consonant chord of all the voices in the Church, including those that presently are somewhat dissonant.

Our topic is not "The Church's Teaching concerning the Family."[1] The topic is "The Gospel of the Family." In this way, we return to the source from which that teaching has originated. Already the Council of Trent said that the gospel, which is believed and lived in the church, is the source of every saving truth and the discipline of morals (DH 1501; cf. EG 36). That means that the church's teaching is not a stagnant lagoon, but a stream, originating from the fountainhead of the gospel, into which the faith experience of the people of God from every century is received. It is a living tradition, which today—as was frequently the case in history—has arrived at a critical point and, with an eye to the "signs of the times" (GS 4), calls for further development and deepening.[2] What is this gospel? It is not a code of law. It is the light and the power of life, which is Jesus Christ; it bestows what it requires. The commandments are comprehensible and able to be fulfilled only in his light and in his power. According to Thomas Aquinas, the law of the new covenant is not a *lex scripta* [written law], but rather the *gratia Spiritus Sancti, quae datur per fidem Christi* [the grace of the Holy Spirit, which is given through faith in Christ]. Without the Spirit active in our hearts, the letter of the gospel is a law that kills (2 Cor 3:6).[3] Therefore, the gospel of the family does not intend to be a burden, but rather, as a gift of faith, it intends to be the light and power of family life. In this way, we have come to the central point. The sacraments, including the sacrament of marriage, are sacraments of faith. *Signa protestantia fidem* [signs bearing witness to faith], Thomas Aquinas says.[4] The Second Vatican Council reinforces this statement. Concerning the sacraments, it says, "They not only presuppose faith, but...they also nourish, strengthen, and express it" (SC 59). The sacrament of marriage too can be effective and can be lived only in faith. The central question, therefore, is, how is the faith of the engaged couple and the married couple doing? In countries with an ancient Christian culture, we experience nowadays the disintegration of the self-evidence of Christian faith and the natural law understanding of marriage and family, which had been valid for many centuries. Many today are baptized, but not evangelized. Formulated paradoxically: they are baptized catechumens or even baptized pagans.

In this situation, we can neither begin with a list of doctrines and commandments, nor can we fix upon the hot-button topics that are mentioned in public discussions. We do not want to circumvent these issues, but we must begin radically, that is, from the roots of faith; we must begin with the basic elements of faith (Heb 5:12) and then traverse the path of faith step-by-step (FC 9, 34; EG 34–39).[5] God is a God of the journey. In the history of salvation, he has walked on the path with us. The church too has walked the path in its history. It must again walk the path today with the people of our day. The church does not want to impose the faith on anyone. The church can only present it and offer it as a path to life's happiness. The gospel can persuade only on its own merits and by means of its inner beauty.

1. THE FAMILY IN THE ORDER OF CREATION

The gospel of the family reaches back to the primordial beginnings of humanity. The creator has given it to humanity for their journey. Thus, esteem for the institution of marriage and family is found in all cultures of the human race. It is understood as a life partnership of man and woman together with their children. This tradition of humanity is found in various manifestations in different cultures. In the beginning, the family was embedded in the extended family or in the clan. Despite all differences in details, the institution of the family is *the* primordial organization in human culture.

All ancient human cultures understood their customs and laws concerning family order as matters of divine ordinance. The existence, well-being, and future of the people depended on their observance. In the context of the Axial Age, the Greeks spoke no longer in mythical terms, but in a somewhat enlightened way of an order that had been established in human nature. Paul took up this way of thinking and spoke of the natural moral law, which was written into the heart of every person by God (Rom 2:14f.) Every culture knows, in one form or another, the Golden Rule, which commands us to treat others as oneself. Jesus confirmed the Golden Rule in the Sermon on the Mount (Matt 7:12; Luke 6:31). In it the commandment to love one's neighbor—to love the other as oneself (Matt 22:39f.)—is embryonically laid out. The Golden Rule is regarded as a summary of the natural law and what the law and the prophets teach (Matt 7:12; 22:40; Luke 6:31).[6] The natural law, which comes to expression in the Golden Rule, enables dialogue with all people of good will. It gives us a criterion for making judgments about polygamy, forced marriage, violence in marriage and family, machismo, discrimination of women, and prostitution, as well as a criterion for making judgments about modern economic conditions and work and pay circumstances that are inimical to families. The decisive question in each case is what—in the relation of man, woman, and children—conforms to respect for the dignity of the other person.

As useful as the natural law is, it remains general and is ambiguous when it comes to concrete questions. In this situation, God has provided us accommodation by means of revelation. Revelation has concretely interpreted what we can recognize according to natural law. The Old Testament proceeded from the traditional wisdom of the ancient Orient at that time and gradually purified and perfected it, through a long process of development, in light of its faith in Yahweh. The second tablet of the Decalogue (Exod 20:12–17; Deut 5:16–21) is the result of this process. Jesus affirmed it (Matt 19:18f.) and the church fathers were convinced that the commandments of the second tablet of the Decalogue concur with the commandments that derive from the moral consciousness common to all people. The commandments of the second tablet of the Decalogue are, accordingly, not a unique Judeo-Christian code of morality. They are the concretized tradition of humanity. In them, the fundamental values of family life are placed under the special protection of God: deep respect for parents and care for elderly parents, the inviolability of marriage, the protection of new human life that proceeds from marriage, and property as the foundation of existence for the family and for truthful dealings with one another, without which no community can exist.

With these commandments, humanity has been given a set of guiding principles and, so to speak, a compass to take along its way. For this reason, the Bible does not understand these commandments as a burden upon or restriction of freedom; it rejoices in God's commandments (Pss 1:2; 112:1; 199). They are signposts on the path to a happy and fulfilled life. One cannot impose them on anyone, but can offer them to everyone, with good reasons, as a path to happiness.

The gospel of the family in the Old Testament has come to its conclusion in the first two chapters of Genesis. They too contain the primordial heritage of humanity, critically interpreted and deepened in light of faith in Yahweh. In the formation of the canon of the Bible, they were put up front, altogether programmatically, as an aid to reading and interpretation. In them we are presented with God's original plan of creation with regard to the family. Three fundamental statements emerge:

> So God created humankind in his image,
> in the image of God he created them;
> male and female he created them. (Gen 1:27)

The human being, with its two sexes, is God's good—indeed, very good—creation. The human being is not created as a single entity. "It is not good that the man should be alone; I will make him a helper as his partner" (2:18) Therefore, Adam greets the woman with a jubilant word of welcome (2:23). Man and woman are given to and for each other as a gift from God. They should mutually complement and support each other and should experience joy and delight in each other.

As an image of God, both—man and woman—have the same dignity. There is no place for the discrimination of women. But man and woman are not simply identical. Their equality in dignity, as well as their difference, is grounded in creation. Both equality and difference are given to them neither by themselves nor by someone else. One does not become a man or a woman by means of the socialization process of the prevailing culture, as some forms of feminism claim.[7] Being man and being woman are ontologically grounded in creation. The equal dignity of their difference establishes the attraction between them, which is extolled in the myths and in the great poetry of humankind, as in the Song of Songs in the Old Testament. Ideological leveling of their difference destroys erotic love. The Bible understands this love as becoming one flesh, that is, a life partnership that includes sex and eros as well as human friendship (Gen 2:24). In this comprehensive sense, man and woman are created for love and therein are an image of God, who is love (1 John 4:8). As a reflection of God, human love is something great and beautiful, but it is not itself divine. The Bible demythologizes the ancient Oriental banalization of sexuality in temple prostitution and condemns debauchery as idolatry. If a partner idolizes the other and expects that the other will prepare heaven on earth for him or her, then the other is necessarily overwhelmed and can only disappoint. Many marriages fail because of this excessive expectation. The life partnership of man and woman, together with their children, can only be happy if it is understood as a gift that points beyond itself. Thus, the creation of the human being flows into the seventh day of creation, into the celebration of the Sabbath. The human being is not created as a work-horse, but is created for the Sabbath. The Sabbath is supposed to be a day of being available for God, and also a day of being available for feasting and celebrating together, a day of leisure with and for each other (see Exod 20:8–10; Deut 5:12–14). We should learn anew from our Jewish friends that the Sabbath, respectively Sunday, is a day for family.

"God blessed them, and God said to them,
'Be fruitful and multiply.'" (Gen 1:28)

The love between man and woman does not simply revolve around itself; it transcends and objectifies itself in children, who proceed from their love. The love between man and woman and the passing on of life belong together. That is true not only for the act of procreation, but stretches beyond that. The first biological birth is carried forward in the second, in the social and cultural birth, in the introduction to life and by passing on life's values. For that, children need protective space and affective security in the love of parents; on the other hand, children strengthen and enrich the bond of love between parents. Children are a joy and not a burden.

For the Bible, fertility is no purely biological reality. Children are the fruit of God's blessing. That blessing is

God's power in history and in the future. Creation's blessing continues in the promise of Abraham's offspring (Gen 12:2f.; 18:18; 22:18). In this way, the vital power of fertility, which was deified in the ancient world, is integrated into the historical activity of God. God places the future of the people and the continuing existence of humankind in the hands of man and woman. Talk about responsible parenthood has a deeper meaning than what is usually given it. It means that God hands over the most valuable thing he can bestow— human life—to the responsibility of man and woman. They may responsibly decide the number and the rhythm of the birth of their children. They are supposed to do that in responsibility before God and with respect for the dignity and well-being of their partner, in responsibility for the welfare of their children, in responsibility for the future of society, and with deep respect for the nature of human beings (GS 50). From this ensues no casuistry, but indeed a binding gestalt of meaning, whose concrete realization is entrusted to the responsibility of man and woman.[8] Responsibility for the future is entrusted to them. The future of humanity transpires because of and with the family. Without family, there is no future, but rather a senescence of society—a danger before which Western societies stand.

"Fill the earth and subdue it." (Gen 1:28)

The words *subdue* and *have dominion* have sometimes been understood in the sense of a violent subjugation and exploitation, and sometimes Christianity has been blamed for our environmental problems. Biblical scholars have shown that one must not understand the two words in the sense of violent subjugation and dominion. The second story of creation speaks of cultivating and tending (2:15). What we are dealing with here, as we say today, is humanity's cultural mandate. Humans are supposed to care for and cherish the earth like a garden; we are supposed to be shepherds of the world, shaping it into a humane environment. This mission is assigned in common to man and woman. Not only human life, but the earth in its totality is consigned to their care and responsibility.

With this cultural mandate, the relation of man and woman once again points beyond itself. Their love is not a form of sentimentality revolving around itself; their love is not to be shut up within itself, but rather should be open to a mission for the world. The family is not only a private, personal community. It is the fundamental and living cell of society. It is the school of humanity and the school of social virtues, which are necessary for life and the development of society (GS 47, 52). It is essential for the emergence of a civilization of love[9] and for the humanizing and personalizing of society, without which society becomes an anonymous mass. In this sense, one can speak of the family's social and political mission (FC 44).

The family, as a primordial institution of humankind, is older than the state and is an institution in its own right in relation to the state. In the order of creation, there is not a single word about the state. The state is supposed to support and promote the family to the best of its abilities; it may not, however, intrude upon the family's own rights. The rights of the family, which are spelled out in the Charter of Rights of the Family, are grounded in the order of creation (FC 46). The family, as the basic cell of state and society, is at the same time the foundational model for the state and for humankind as one human family.[10] From this consequences follow for the kind of family order needed for the just distribution of goods and for peace in the world (EG 176–258). The gospel of the family is at the same time a gospel for the well-being and peace of humankind.

2. STRUCTURES OF SIN IN THE LIFE OF THE FAMILY

What has been previously said is an ideal picture, but it simply is not the reality of families. The Bible knows that as well. Thus, chapter 3, with the expulsion from paradise and from the paradisaical reality of marriage and family, follows chapters 1 and 2 of Genesis. The alienation of human beings from God has as a consequence alienation in and among human beings. In the language of the theological tradition, we call this alienation concupiscence, by which we ought not understand only disordered sexual desires. In order to avoid this misunderstanding, nowadays we often speak of structures of sin (FC 9). They encumber the life of the family too. The Bible gives a realistic description of the *conditio humana* [human condition] and its interpretation from the perspective of faith. The first alienation happens between man and woman. They feel shame in front of each other (Gen 3:10f.). Shame shows that the original harmony of body and spirit is disturbed and that man and woman are alienated from one another. Affectionate inclination degenerates into mutual lust and the domination of man over woman (3:16). They mutually reproach and blame each other (3:12). It ends up in violence, jealousy, and discord in marriage and the family.

The second alienation affects women and mothers in a

special way. They must now bear their children with travail and pain (Gen 3:16). With pain, they must also raise their children. How many mothers cry and wail because of their children, just like Rachel wept for her children and could not be comforted (Jer 31:15; Matt 2:18)? The alienation also affects the relation of human beings to nature and the world. The world is no longer the beautiful garden; it bears only thorns and thistles; it is unruly and resistant; work has become hard and arduous. Man must now pursue work with travail and with the sweat of his brow (Gen 3:19).

It soon comes to alienation and strife in the family too. It comes to envy and strife between brothers, to war between brothers, and even to murder of one's brother (Gen 4:1–16). The Bible reports infidelity between marriage partners, which reaches even into Jesus' family tree. There two women (Tamar and the wife of Uriah) appear who are regarded as sinners (Matt 1:3f.) Even Jesus had ancestors who were not from "a good house," and whom one would prefer to hide and keep silent about. Here the Bible is totally realistic, entirely honest.

Finally, there is the most fundamental alienation of death (Gen 3:19; cf. Rom 5:12) and all the forces of death, which rage in the world and bring calamity, death, and perdition. They also bring suffering into the family. Let us merely think about how it is when mothers stand by the casket of their children or when spouses have to take their leave from one another, which hits happy marriages especially hard and entails painful years of loneliness for many older people.

When we speak of the family and of the beauty of family, we may not proceed from an unrealistic, romantic ideal picture. We must also see the hard realities and share the sorrow, the worries, and the tears of many families. Biblical realism can, in fact, provide a certain solace. It shows us that what we bemoan today is not something that occurs nowadays for the first time; in principle, it was always this way. We may not succumb to the temptation to romanticize the past and then, as is fashionable in many circles, view the present as a story of total decay. Praise of the good old days and complaints about the younger generation have been around ever since there has been an older generation. Not only is the Church a field hospital (as Pope Francis has said), the family too is a field hospital, where it is necessary to bind many wounds, dry many tears, and establish reconciliation and peace time and again. In the end, the third chapter of Genesis turns on a light of hope. With the expulsion from paradise, God gave human beings a hope to take along on their journey. What the tradition describes as a protogospel (Gen 3:15) can also be understood as a protogospel of the family. The savior will come from their progeny. The genealogies in Matthew and Luke (Matt 1:1–17; Luke 3:23–38) testify that the savior finally has come from this genealogical line, even if it ran a bumpy course. God can write straight even with crooked lines. As people's companions, we should, therefore, not be prophets of doom, but rather bearers of hope, who dispense solace and give courage for carrying on even in difficult situations.

3. THE FAMILY IN THE CHRISTIAN ORDER OF SALVATION

Jesus joined a family history. He grew up in the family of Nazareth (Luke 2:51f.) To it belonged also brothers and sisters in the broader sense (Mark 3:31–33; 6:3) as well as distant, yet obviously intimate relatives like Elizabeth, Zachary, and John the Baptist (Luke 1:36, 39–56). At the beginning of his public ministry, Jesus participated in the celebration of the wedding at Cana and performed his first sign there (John 2:1–12). In the process, he placed his entire ministry under the sign of a wedding and its accompanying joy. With him—the bridegroom (Matt 9:15)—the eschatological wedding and joyful time that was promised by the prophets has dawned.

A fundamental statement by Jesus concerning marriage and family is found in his famous words about divorce (Matt 19:3–9). Moses had permitted divorce under certain conditions (Deut 24:1). The conditions were debated among the different schools of Jewish scribes. Jesus does not engage in this casuistry. He appeals to the original will of God: "At the beginning of creation, it was not so."[11] The disciples are shocked at this statement. To them it appears to be an unheard-of attack on the surrounding world's conception of marriage, as well as a pitiless and excessive demand. "If such is the case of a man with his wife, it is better not to marry." Jesus indirectly confirms that, viewed from a human perspective, this is an excessive demand. It must be "given" to human beings; it is a gift of grace.

The expression "given" shows that we must not isolate Jesus' words, but rather must understand them in the total context of his message about the kingdom of God. Jesus attributes divorce to hard-heartedness (Matt 19:8), which shuts one off from God and others. With the coming of the kingdom of God, the prediction of the prophets has been fulfilled, according to which God, in the messianic age, will transform the hard heart into a new heart, which is no longer hard like a stone, but is a heart of flesh, which is soft, empathetic, and compassionate (Ezek 36:26f.; cf. Jer 31:33; Ps 51:12). So just as adultery begins in the heart (Matt 5:28), so too the cure is possible only through conversion and through the gift of a new heart. For this reason, Jesus distanced himself from the hard-heartedness and hypocrisy of the draconian punishments imposed upon an adulteress, and he forgave a woman accused of adultery (John 8:2–11; cf. Luke 7:36–50).

Jesus' good news is that the covenant, which the spouses establish, is embraced and borne by God's covenant, which continues to exist even when the fragile human bond of love becomes weaker or even dies. God's definitive and indissoluble pledge of fidelity and covenant removes caprice from the human covenant, lending it stability and endurance. The bond that God places on the spouses would be falsely understood if one wanted to understand it as a yoke. It is God's humane pledge of fidelity; it is encouragement and an ever-new source of strength for maintaining fidelity to one another in the midst of life's vicissitudes. From this message, Augustine derived the teaching concerning the indissoluble bond of marriage, which continues to exist even when the marriage, on the human plane, falls apart.[12] To many nowadays that teaching is scarcely intelligible. One ought not understand this teaching as a kind of metaphysical hypostasis beside or over the personal love of the spouses; on the other hand, it is not totally absorbed in their affective, mutual love, nor does it die with it (GS 48; EG 66). It is good news, that is, definitive solace and a pledge that continues to be valid. As such it takes the human person and his or her freedom seriously. It is the dignity of the human person to be able to make permanent decisions. They belong enduringly to the person's history; they mark him or her in a lasting way; one cannot simply cast them off or undo them. If those decisions of commitment are broken, then that signifies a deep wound. Wounds can heal. The scar remains and frequently causes pain, but one can and may go on living, even though it may be difficult. It is similar with Jesus' good news: because of God's mercy, forgiveness, healing, and a new beginning are possible for the one who experiences conversion.

Paul takes up Jesus' message. He speaks of a marriage "in the Lord" (1 Cor 7:39). An ecclesial form of marriage ceremony is not meant. Such a thing evolved only centuries later, definitively only by means of the decretal *Tametsi* of the Council of Trent (1563). The "household codes" (Col 3:18—4:1; Eph 5:21—6:9; 1 Pet 2:18—3:7) show that this "in the Lord" encompasses all aspects of life in the family: the relation of man and woman, of parents and children, of masters and slaves living in the house. The domestic codes assimilate patriarchal house rules, but modify them "in the Lord." They are examples of the norm-altering and norm-making power of Christian faith. Because of them, out of the one-sided subordination of woman to man a mutual relationship of love develops, which should stamp all of the other family relationships. Paul in fact says what was unique, indeed revolutionary in the entire ancient world, that the difference between man and woman no longer counts for those who are "one in Christ" (Gal 3:28).

The Letter to the Ephesians goes a step further. It takes up the Old Testament metaphor of the marriage covenant, which is especially evidenced in Hosea (Hos 2:18–25), as an expression of God's covenant with his people. This covenant found its fulfillment and completion in Christ. Thus, the covenant of man and woman now becomes a real symbol for God's covenant with human beings, which was fulfilled in Jesus Christ. What was, from the very beginning of the world, a reality of God's good creation now becomes a sign that makes visible the mystery of Christ and the Church (Eph 5:32). On the basis of a theological-historical development that only came to a conclusion in the twelfth century, the Council of Trent saw in this statement an indication of the sacramentality of marriage (DH 1799; cf. DH 1327). More recent theology seeks to deepen this christological foundation in a trinitarian way; it understands the family as a truly symbolic illustration of the mystery of trinitarian *communio* [communion].

As a sacrament, marriage is both a remedy for the consequences of sin as well as a means of sanctifying grace. One can transfer this teaching to the family and say that by entering into the history of a family, Jesus healed the family and sanctified it. The order of salvation takes up the order of creation. It is not inimical to the body or sexuality; it includes sex, eros, and human friendship; it purifies and perfects them. Similar to the holiness of the Church, the holiness of the family is also no static entity. It is repeatedly threatened by hard-heartedness. Time and again it must go the way of conversion, renewal, and maturation anew. Just as the Church is underway on the path of conversion and renewal (LG 8), so too marriage and the family, on the path of cross and resurrection (FC 12f.), stand under the law of gradual development—of growing into the mystery of Christ in a repeatedly new and deeper way (FC 9, 34).

Time and again the new heart demands nobleness of

heart and presupposes a culture of heart. Family life desires to be cultivated according to the three key phrases of the Holy Father: "May I?", "thank you," and "I'm sorry." One must have time for each other; celebrate the Sabbath with each other; and repeatedly practice forbearance, forgiveness, and patience. Signs of benevolence, appreciation, tenderness, gratitude, and love are necessary time and again. Praying together, receiving the sacrament of reconciliation, and celebrating the Eucharist together are aids for repeatedly strengthening anew the bond of marriage, which God has placed on the spouses. It is always something beautiful to meet elderly spouses who, even at an advanced age, are still in love in a mature way. This too is a sign of redeemed humanity. The Bible concludes with the vision of the eschatological wedding of the lamb (Rev 19:7, 9). Marriage and family thereby become an eschatological symbol. With the earthly wedding celebration, the eschatological wedding is celebrated in an anticipatory way. Therefore, it should be observed in a splendid and festive way.

As eschatological anticipation, the earthly wedding is at the same time relativized. Jesus himself was unmarried, which was unusual for a rabbi, and, for the sake of discipleship, he demanded a readiness to forsake marriage and family (Matt 10:37) and, from those to whom the gift was given, celibacy for the sake of the kingdom of heaven (Matt 9:12). For Paul, celibacy is the better way in a world that is passing away. It grants the freedom to be undivided in attending to the affairs of the Lord (1 Cor 7:25–38). Because celibacy has become a recognized, freely chosen estate in its own right, marriage too is no longer a matter of social compulsion, but rather a free choice. Either marriage and celibacy valorize and support each other, or both of them together fall into crisis, as we unfortunately experience it in the present.

We are in this crisis. The gospel of marriage and the family is no longer intelligible to many. For many it does not appear to be a livable option in their situation. What are we to do? Little is to be accomplished with good words alone. Jesus shows us a more realistic way. He says to us that no Christian is ever alone or lost, whether married or single, whether abandoned by one's partner, or as a child or young person growing up without contact to his or her own family. He or she is at home in a new family of brothers and sisters (Matt 12:48–50; 19:27–29). The gospel of the family becomes concrete in the domestic church; in it, that gospel can become livable again. Today the domestic church is once again relevant.

4. THE FAMILY AS DOMESTIC CHURCH

According to the New Testament, the Church is the house of God (1 Pet 2:5; 4:17; 1 Tim 3:15; Heb 10:21). The liturgy often describes the Church as the *familia Dei* [family of God]. It is supposed to be a house for all; in it everyone should be permitted to feel at home and as belonging in the family. In the ancient world, relatives living in the house, slaves, and often friends or guests also generally belonged to the house, alongside the *paterfamilias* and his wife, together with their children. It is in this context that we must understand it when, concerning the primitive Christian community, we hear that the first Christians came together in houses (Acts 2:26; 5:42). Frequently there is talk of the conversion of entire households (Acts 11:14; 16:15, 31, 33).

In Paul, the Church was arranged in houses, that is, as house churches (Rom 16:5; 1 Cor 16:19; Col 4:15; Phlm 2). For Paul they were a base and point of departure for his missionary trips; they were the foundational center and building block of the local community; they were places of prayer, catechetical instruction, Christian fellowship, and hospitality for traveling Christians. Before Constantine's conversion, they were also in fact a gathering place for the celebration of the Lord's Supper.

Domestic churches have also played a significant role in the subsequent history of the Church; above all, mention is to be made of the Pietist communities and free churches, from whom we can learn in this regard. In Catholic families, there were and still are little house altars (domestic shrines), at which the family gathers for common prayer in the evening or at special times (Advent, Christmas Eve, situations of need or misfortune, etc.). Such customs of popular piety deserve a renewal. One thinks perhaps of customs like the parents' blessing of their children, religious images, above all a cross in the residence, holy water as a reminder of baptismal water, among others.

The Second Vatican Council, following Chrysostom, took the idea of the domestic church up again (LG 11; AA 11).[13] From the brief mention in the documents of the Council detailed chapters have been developed in the postconciliar documents. Above all, Pope Paul VI's apostolic exhortation, *Evangelii Nuntiandi* (1975), has carried the impulse of the Council forward after the Council.[14] It described the ecclesial base communities as hope for the universal Church (EN 58, 71). In Latin America, Africa, Asia (in the Philippines, India, Korea, among others), the domestic churches, in the form of basic Christian communities or as small Christian communities, have become a pastoral recipe for success. Especially in minority and diaspora situations and in situations of persecution, they became a matter of survival for the Church.

In the meantime, the impulses that have come out of Latin America, Africa, and Asia are beginning to bear good fruit in Western civilization. There the old popular Church structures are proving to be less and less viable, pastoral areas are becoming larger, and Christians often become cognitive minorities. In addition, the nuclear family, having freed itself from the earlier extended family beginning in the 18th century, has in the meantime experienced a structural crisis. Modern working and living conditions have led to a separation of residence, work place, and locations for recreational activities, thereby contributing to the collapse of the house as a social unit. For professional reasons, fathers must often be absent from their families for a longer time. Wives too, because of their professional work, are often only minimally present in the family. Because of the conditions of modern life that are inimical to families, the modern nuclear family has encountered difficulties. Even people who do not live on the street have become, in a deeper sense, homeless and without shelter in the anonymous milieu of big cities, especially on the bleak peripheries of modern megalopolises. We must build new houses for them, in the literal and in the figurative sense. Domestic churches can be an answer. Of course, we cannot simply replicate today the domestic churches of the early church. We need a new kind of extended family. So that nuclear families can survive, they must be embedded in a system of family ties that extends over generations, where especially grandmothers and grandfathers play an important role; they must be embedded in interfamilial circles of friends and neighborhoods, in which children find shelter when their parents are absent and in which single older people, divorced individuals, and single parents feel somewhat at home. Apostolic and spiritual communities often provide the spiritual space and spiritual atmosphere for communities of families. The rudiments of domestic churches are found in prayer groups, Bible groups, catechetical groups, and ecumenical groups, among others. Domestic churches are an *ecclesiola in ecclesia*, a small church within the big Church. They make the Church present on site in the midst of life. For where two or three are gathered in Christ's name, he is there in their midst (Matt 18:20). On the basis of baptism and confirmation, house communities are the messianic people of God (LG 9). They participate in the priestly, prophetic, and royal priesthood (1 Pet 2:8; Rev 1:6; 5:10. Cf. LG 10–12, 30–38). Through the Holy Spirit, the *sensus fidei*, the sense of faith, is intrinsic in them—an intuitive sense for the faith and for a praxis of life that conforms to the gospel. Domestic communities are not only the object, but also the subject of family pastoral care. Above all through their example, they can help the Church to penetrate more deeply into the word of God and to apply it more fully in life (LG 12, 35; EG 154f.). Because the Holy Spirit is given to the Church as a whole, they should not isolate themselves in sectarian fashion from the larger *communio* of the Church (EN 58, 64; EG 29). This "Catholic principle" preserves the Church from collapsing into individual, autonomous free churches. By means of such unity in diversity, the Church is, so to speak, a sacramental sign of unity in the world (LG 1, 9).

Domestic churches foster the sharing of the Bible. From God's word they create light and strength for daily living (DV 25; EG 152f.) In view of the rupture in passing on the faith to the next generation (EG 70), they have the important catechetical task of leading people to the joy of the gospel.[15] They pray together for their own concerns and the concerns of the world. Together with the entire community, they should celebrate the Sunday Eucharist as the source and summit of the whole Christian life (LG 11).[16] In the family circle, they observe the day of the Lord as a day of leisure, joy, and togetherness, just as they observe the times of the liturgical year with its rich customs (SC 102–11). They are places of community spirituality, in which one accepts each other in the spirit of love, forgiveness, and reconciliation; in which one shares the good times and the bad, the cares, the needs and sorrows, the joy and human happiness in daily living, on Sunday and holidays.[17] By all these means, they build up the body of the Church (LG 41). The Church, according to its essence, is missionary (AG 2); to evangelize is its deepest identity (EN 14, 59). Families, as domestic churches, are called upon in a special way to pass on the faith in their respective milieu. They have their own missionary and prophetic mission. Their witness is primarily the witness of life, through which they can, as it were, work like yeast in the world (Matt 13:33; cf. AA 2–8; EN 21, 41, 71, 76; EG 119–21). Just as Christ came to proclaim the good news to the poor (Luke 4:18; Matt 11:5) and to bless the poor and the sorrowful, the little ones and the children (Matt 5:3f.; 11:25; Luke

6:20f.), so too did he send his disciples out to proclaim the good news to the poor (Luke 7:22). For this reason, domestic churches may not be exclusive, elite communities. They must be open to the needy of every sort, to the simple and little people. They should know that the kingdom of God belongs to the children (Mark 10:14; cf. EG 197–201).

Families need the Church and the Church needs families in order to be present in the midst of life and in the milieus of modern living. Without domestic churches, the Church is estranged from the concrete reality of life. Only through families can the Church be at home there, where people are at home. Understanding the Church as a domestic church is, therefore, fundamental for the future of the Church and for the new evangelization. Families are the first and the best messengers of the gospel of the family. They are the way of the Church.

5. CONCERNING THE PROBLEM OF THE DIVORCED AND REMARRIED

When one thinks about the meaning of families for the future of the Church, then the rapidly increasing number of broken families is all the more a tragedy. Everyone knows: the problem of the divorced and remarried is a complex and thorny problem. One may not reduce the problem to the question of admission to communion. It touches upon pastoral care for marriage and family life in their totality. It begins already with pastoral care for youth and with marriage preparation, which should be a thorough catechesis for marriage and family life. The task continues with the pastoral accompaniment of married couples and families. It becomes relevant and immediate when a marriage or a family is plunged into a crisis. In this situation, pastoral ministers will do everything possible to contribute to healing and reconciling the marriage and the family that has fallen into crisis.

Everyone, however, also knows that there are situations in which every reasonable attempt to save a marriage proves to be in vain. One will marvel at and support the heroism of partners who have been abandoned, who remain alone and who struggle through life alone. However, many deserted partners, for the sake of the children, are dependent upon a new partnership and a civil marriage, which they cannot again quit without new guilt. In such new ties they often experience human happiness—indeed a virtual gift from heaven—after previous bitter experiences. What can the Church do in such situations? It cannot propose a solution apart from or contrary to Jesus' words. The indissolubility of a sacramental marriage and the impossibility of contracting a second sacramental marriage during the lifetime of the other partner is a binding part of the Church's faith tradition, which one cannot repeal or water down by appealing to a superficially understood and cheapened sense of mercy. God's fidelity is ultimately the fidelity of God to himself and to his love. Because God is faithful, he is also merciful and, in his mercy, he is faithful, even when we are unfaithful (2 Tim 2:13). Mercy and fidelity belong together. Therefore, there can be no human situation that is absolutely desperate and hopeless. However far a human being may fall, he or she never falls deeper than God's mercy can reach.

The question, therefore, is how the Church can conform to this indissoluble cohesiveness of fidelity and mercy in its pastoral practice with civilly remarried, divorced people. This is a relatively recent problem, which first emerged since the introduction of civil marriage in Napoleon's Civil Code (1804) and its successive introduction in different countries. The reaction of the Church to this new situation has made important progress. The 1917 Code of Canon Law (c. 2356) still treats the civilly divorced and remarried as bigamists, who—ipso facto—are dishonorable and who, according to the seriousness of their guilt, can be excommunicated or placed under personal interdict. The 1983 Code of Canon Law (c. 1093) no longer contains these threats of punishment; what remain are less severe restrictions. In the meantime, *Familiaris Consortio* (84) and *Sacramentum Caritatis* (29) speak well-nigh lovingly of such Christians. These documents assure them that they belong to the Church and are invited to participate in the life of the Church. That is a new tone.

We find ourselves in a situation similar to that of the last council, when it dealt with the issues of ecumenism and religious freedom. Then too there were encyclicals and decisions of the Holy Office, which appeared to block wider paths. Without violating the binding dogmatic tradition, the council opened doors. Therefore, one can ask: Is not a further development possible with regard to our issue too—a development that does not repeal the binding faith tradition, but carries forward and deepens more recent traditions?

The answer can only be a nuanced one. For the situations are very different and must be carefully differentiated (FC 84). For this reason, there cannot be a general solution for all cases. I will limit myself to two situations, for which solutions are already mentioned in the official documents. In the process, I want only to pose questions and indicate the direction of possible answers. The Synod will have to give the definitive answer itself.

First situation. *Familiaris Consortio* says that some of the divorced and remarried are subjectively convinced in conscience that their irreparably broken, previous marriage was never valid (FC 84). Many pastors are in fact convinced that many marriages, which were concluded in ecclesial form, are not validly contracted. For as a sacrament of faith, marriage presupposes faith and consent to the essential characteristics of marriage—unity and indissolubility. But can we, in the present situation, presuppose without further ado that the engaged couple shares the belief in the mystery that is signified by the sacrament and that they really understand and affirm the canonical conditions for the validity of their marriage? Is not the *praesumptio iuris* [presumption of validity], from which canon law proceeds, often a *fictio iuris* [legal fiction]?

Because marriage as a sacrament has a public character, the decision about the validity of a marriage cannot simply be left to the subjective judgment of the parties concerned. However, one can ask whether the juridical path, which is in fact not *iure divino* [by divine law], but has developed in the course of history, can be the only path to the resolution of the problem, or whether other, more pastoral and spiritual procedures are conceivable. Alternatively, one might imagine that the bishop could entrust this task to a priest with spiritual and pastoral experience as a penitentiary or episcopal vicar. Independent of the answer to this question, it is worthwhile to recall the address that Pope Francis delivered on January 24, 2014, to the members of the Roman Rota, in which he emphasized that the juridical and the pastoral dimensions are not in opposition to each other. On the contrary, the ecclesial system of law has an essential pastoral character. One must, therefore, ask: What does pastoral mean? Certainly not simply indulgence, which would be a false understanding both of pastoral care and of mercy. Mercy does not exclude justice; it is no cheap grace or a kind of clearance sale. Pastoral care and mercy are not contradictory to justice, but are, so to speak, the higher righteousness because behind every individual legal appeal stands not only a case that can be viewed through the lens of a general rule, but rather a human person, who is not only a case, but rather a being who possesses unique personal dignity. That makes necessary a hermeneutic that is juridical and pastoral and that applies a general law with prudence and wisdom, according to justice and fairness, to a concrete, often complex situation. Or as Pope Francis has said: a hermeneutic that is inspired by the love of the Good Shepherd and that sees that behind every process, behind every case stand persons who expect justice. Therefore, can it really be that decisions are made about the weal and woe of people at a second and a third hearing only on the basis of records, that is, on the basis of paper, but without knowledge of the persons and their situation?

Second situation. It would be mistaken to seek the resolution of the problem in a generous expansion of the annulment process. The disastrous impression would thereby be created that the Church is proceeding in a dishonest way by granting what, in reality, are divorces. We must also keep in mind situations of a valid and consummated marriage between baptized individuals, for whom the marital life partnership is irreparably broken and one or both partners have contracted a second, civil marriage.

The Congregation for the Doctrine of the Faith provided a guideline already in 1994 when it declared—and Benedict XVI reiterated it at the World Meeting of Families in Milan in 2012—that the divorced and remarried admittedly cannot receive sacramental communion, but can indeed receive spiritual communion. Many will be grateful for this statement. But it also raises questions. For the one who receives spiritual communion is one with Jesus Christ. How can he or she then be in contradiction to Christ's commandment? Why, then, can't he or she also receive sacramental communion? If we exclude divorced and remarried Christians, who are properly disposed, from the sacraments and refer them to the extrasacramental way of salvation, do we not then place the fundamental sacramental structure of the Church in question? Wherefore then the Church? Do we not then pay too high a price? Some argue that it is precisely nonparticipation in communion that demonstrates the sanctity of the sacrament. The counterquestion is: Does that not exploit a human being, if we make him or her into a sign for others, when he or she cries for help? Are we going to let him or her starve sacramentally so that others may live?

The early church gives us a suggestion that can serve as a way out of the dilemma, to which Professor Joseph Ratzinger referred already in 1972.[18] Very early on the Church experienced that even apostasy happens among Christians. During persecutions, there were Christians who became weak and denied their baptism. For such *lapsi* [lapsed Christians], the Church developed the canonical praxis of penance as a second baptism, not by means of water, but by means of the tears of repentance. After the shipwreck of sin, not a second ship, but a lifesaving plank should be made available to the drowning person.[19]

In a similar way, there was also hardness of heart among Christians (Matt 19:8) and cases of adultery with a subsequent, second, quasi-marital liaison. The response of the church fathers was not uniform. So much is nevertheless certain, that in individual local churches there existed the customary law, according to which Christians, who were living in a second relationship during the lifetime of the first partner, had available to them, after a period of penance, admittedly no second ship—no second marriage—but indeed a plank of salvation through participation in communion. Origen reports on this custom and describes it as "not unreasonable." Basil the Great and Gregory of Nazianzus referred to this praxis too. Even Augustine himself, who was otherwise strict in this matter, appears, at least in one passage, not to have excluded every pastoral solution. Out of pastoral concern "to prevent something worse," these fathers were willing to tolerate something that, in itself, is unacceptable. There was, therefore, a pastoral practice of tolerance, clemency, and forbearance, and there are good reasons for assuming that this praxis was confirmed by the Council of Nicaea (325) against the rigorism of the Novatianists.[20]

As is generally the case, experts dispute the historical details in these matters. In its decisions, the Church cannot commit itself to one or the other position. Nevertheless, independent of the particular questions that are always debated, it is basically clear that the Church repeatedly sought a way beyond both rigorism and laxity and, in the process, appealed to its authority to bind and to loose, which was conferred on her by the Lord (Matt 16:19; 18:18; John 20:23). In the Creed, we confess, *Credo in remissionem peccatorum* [I believe in the forgiveness of sins.] That means that for the one who repents, forgiveness is possible. If forgiveness is possible for the murderer, then it is also possible for the adulterer. Repentance and the sacrament of penance are the way to bind both aspects together: obligation to the word of the Lord and to the never-ending mercy of God. The mercy of God, thus understood, is no cheap grace, which dispenses with conversion. On the other hand, the sacraments are not a reward for good conduct or for an elite, who exclude those who are most in need of them (EG 47).

The question that confronts us is this: Is this path beyond rigorism and laxity, the path of conversion, which issues forth in the sacrament of mercy—the sacrament of penance—also the path that we can follow in this matter? Certainly not in every case. But if a divorced and remarried person is truly sorry that he or she failed in the first marriage, if the commitments from the first marriage are clarified and a return is definitively out of the question, if he or she cannot undo the commitments that were assumed in the second civil marriage without new guilt, if he or she strives to the best of his or her abilities to live out the second civil marriage on the basis of faith and to raise their children in the faith, if he or she longs for the sacraments as a source of strength in his or her situation, do we then have to refuse or can we refuse him or her the sacrament of penance and communion, after a period of reorientation?

The path in question would not be a general solution. It is not a broad path for the great masses, but a narrow path for the indeed smaller segment of divorced and remarried individuals who are honestly interested in the sacraments. Is it not necessary precisely here to prevent something worse? For when children in the families of the divorced and remarried never see their parents go to the sacraments, then they too normally will not find their way to confession and communion. Do we then accept as a consequence that we will also lose the next generation and perhaps the generation after that? Does not our well-preserved praxis then become counterproductive?

On the part of the Church, this path presupposes *discretio*, spiritual discrimination, pastoral prudence, and wisdom. For the monastic father Benedict, *discretio* [discernment] was the mother of all virtues and the basic virtue of the abbot.[21] That is equally true for the bishop. Such *discretio* is no cheap compromise between the extremes of rigorism and laxity, but rather—like every virtue—the path of the responsible middle and the right measure.[22] I hope that, on the path of such *discretio* in the course of the synodal process, we find an answer so that we can credibly bear witness to the word of God in difficult human situations as a message of fidelity, but equally as a message of mercy, life, and joy.

CONCLUSION

With that, I return to the topic "The Gospel of the Family." We may not limit the discussion to the situation of the divorced and remarried or to many other difficult pastoral situations that have not been mentioned in this context. We must begin positively, discovering and proclaiming again the gospel of the family in its total beauty. Truth persuades by means of its beauty. Through word and deed, we must help to ensure that people find their life's happiness in the family and thereby can give to other families a testimony of their happiness. We must once again understand the family as a domestic church and make it the paramount path of the new evangelization as well as the paramount path for the renewal of the Church—a church that is on its way with the people.

Human beings are at home in families, or at least they seek to be at home in a family. In families, the Church encounters the reality of life. Therefore, families are the test case for pastoral care and the most serious test case for the new evangelization. The family is the future. For the Church too, it is the way into the future.

EXCURSUS 1: IMPLICIT FAITH

This pedagogy of God is a constant topic of the church fathers (Clement of Alexandria, Irenaeus of Lyons, among others). The scholastic tradition developed the teaching of *fides implicita* [implicit faith]. It derives from the Letter to the Hebrews 11:1, 6: "Faith is the assurance of things hoped for....Whoever would approach [God] must believe that he exists and that he rewards those who seek him."

For Thomas Aquinas, faith in God is the real content of faith. For him, faith in God as the goal and ultimate happiness of human beings, as well as faith in divine providence throughout history, make up those truths of faith that are the very conduits of salvation; such truths also implicitly include the incarnation and the sufferings of Christ.[23] Even when Thomas, in other passages, varies in the enumeration of the truths of faith that are necessary for salvation (for example,

Summa Theologiae q. 1, a. 6 ad 1), one can regard this statement as his central declaration concerning the topic of implicit faith.[24] So the thesis that it is sufficient for the validity of marriage to intend to contract a marriage the way Christians do falls short of this minimal requirement. For those who are merely cultural Christians, that kind of intention only involves the intent to contract their marriage according to the usual rite of the Church, which many want—not for the sake of the faith—but rather on account of the greater solemnity and festiveness of the church wedding ceremony, in comparison to the civil marriage service.

For the effectiveness of the sacrament, it is indispensable to have faith in the living God as the goal and felicity of humankind and to believe in his providence—that is, faith in the God who wants to lead us on our life's way to the goal and felicity of life. Proceeding from this initial, but foundational faith conviction, as the minimal condition for an effective reception of the sacrament, catechetical instruction in preparation for the church marriage service should show how God has made concretely manifest in us this goal and Jesus Christ as the way to this goal and to life's happiness. It should show how his love and fidelity becomes effectively present through the Church in the sacrament of marriage, in order to accompany the engaged and married couple, together with the children that God will give them, on their future path in life together and to lead them to life's felicity—to life in and with God and, ultimately, to eternal life. In this way, the mystery of Christ and the Church, which becomes concrete in marriage, can gradually be revealed.

EXCURSUS 2: THE PRAXIS OF THE EARLY CHURCH

According to the New Testament, adultery and fornication are behaviors that are in fundamental contradiction to being Christian. Therefore, in the early church, along with apostasy and murder, adultery also belonged to the mortal sins that excluded one from the Church. Because the fornication of one partner, according to the Old Testament–Jewish way of thinking, "contaminates" (Lev 18:25, 28; 19:29; Deut 24:4; Hosea 4:2f.; Jer 3:1–3, 9) the other partner and the entire community, the husband—according to the adultery provisions of Matthew (Matt 5:32 and 19:9), who was writing for Jewish Christians—was permitted, oftentimes even commanded, to leave his adulterous wife. Of course from the very beginning, the church fathers emphasized that the same rights and the same obligations applied to both man and woman. Full clarity about the praxis of the early church concerning release from marriage on account of adultery cannot be obtained from the texts. For the texts do not always clearly distinguish between adultery and fornication, simultaneous and consecutive bigamy after the death of the first partner (even the latter was debated in some cases), and separation because of death or dismissal. Concerning the pertinent exegetical and historical questions, there is a comprehensive, scarcely manageable body of literature as well as differing interpretations. On the one hand, mention should be made of Giovanni Cereti, *Divorzio, Nuove nozze e penitenza nella Chiesa primitive* (Bologna: Edizioni Dehoniane, 2013 [1977]), among others; and on the other hand, Henri Crouzel, *L'Église primitive face au divorce* (Paris: Beauchesne, 1971) and Joseph Ratzinger, "Zur Frage der Unauflöslichkeit der Ehe: Bemerkungen zum dog-mengeschichtlichen Befund und seiner gegenwärtigen Bedeutung," in *Ehe und Ehescheidung*, ed. Franz Heinrich and Volker Eid (Munich: Kösel Verlag, 1972), 35–56.

There can, however, be no doubt about the fact that in the early church there was, according to customary law in many local churches, the praxis of pastoral tolerance, clemency, and forbearance after a period of penance. It is against the background of this practice that canon 8 of the Council of Nicaea (325), which was directed against the rigorism of Novatian, must surely be understood. This customary law is expressly attested to by Origen, who considers it not unreasonable (*Commentary on Matthew*, 14:23). Basil the Great (Letter 188:4 and 199:18), Gregory of Nazianzus (*Oratio* 37) and some others also refer to it. They justify the "not unreasonable" statement with the pastoral intention of "preventing something worse." In the Latin church, this praxis was abandoned upon the authority of Augustine in favor of a stricter praxis. But even Augustine speaks in one passage of a pardonable error (*On Faith and Works*, 19:35) So he too appears not to have excluded every pastoral solution from the outset. Even later, the Western church, with its decisions at synods and the like, repeatedly sought and also found concrete solutions in difficult situations. According to P. Fransen, "Das Thema 'Ehescheidung und Ehebruch' auf dem Konzil von Trient (1563)," *Concilium* 6 (1970): 343–48, the Council of Trent condemned Luther's position, but not the praxis of the Eastern church. Hubert Jedin essentially agreed.

The Orthodox churches preserved the pastoral point of view of the early church tradition, in accordance with their principle of *oikonomia*. However, since the sixth century, following Byzantine imperial law, they have gone beyond the position of pastoral tolerance, clemency, and forbearance and they recognize—besides the provisions concerning adultery—additional grounds for divorce, which are based on the moral and not only the physical death of the marriage bond. The Western church went a different way. It excludes the dissolution of a validly contracted and consummated sacramental marriage between baptized individuals (Code of Canon Law c. 1141). It, however, acknowledges the dissolution of nonconsummated marriages (Code of Canon Law c. 1142) as well as the dissolution of nonsacramental marriages by means of the Pauline or Petrine privilege (Code of Canon Law c. 1143). In addition, there are annulments on account of defects in form. By allowing that, one can ask whether juridical perspectives, which occur very late in history, are not being one-sidedly pushed into the foreground.

Joseph Ratzinger proposed taking up the position of Basil in a new way. That appears to be an appropriate solution, one that also underlies my current reflections. We cannot act on the authority of one or other historical interpretation that is still controversial. A fortiori, we cannot simply replicate the early church's solutions in our situation, which is completely different. In our changed situation, however, we can take up again the early church's fundamental concern and seek to actualize it in today's situation, in a manner that is fair and just in the light of the gospel.

NOTES

1. The most important documents are: Council of Trent: DH 1797–1816; Second Vatican Council, *Gaudium et spes* 47–52 (GS); apostolic exhortation *Familiaris Consortio* (1981) (FC); *Catechism of the Catholic Church* (1993), 1601–66 (CCC); apostolic exhortation *Sacramentum Caritatis* (2007), 27–29; and the encyclical *Lumen Fidei* (2013), 52f.

2. Concerning the development of this teaching: First Vatican Council (DH 3020) and the Second Vatican Council (DV 8). John Henry Newman, *Essay on the Development of Christian Doctrine* (London: James Toovey, 1845). Yves Congar, *Tradition and Traditions: An Historical and a Theological Essay* (New York: Macmillan, 1967).

3. Thomas Aquinas, *Summa Theologiae*, I/II, q. 106, a.1 and 2; cf. EG 37.

4. Thomas Aquinas, *Summa Theologiae*, III, q. 61, a. 4.

5. See excursus 1.

6. Thus the definition of the natural law in the *Decretals of Gratian* (D. 1 d.a.c. 1), which became normative for the natural law tradition of the Middle Ages, and also for the early modern period and older Reformed Christianity.

7. From the distinction between sex, or biological sexuality, and gender, or the social-cultural shaping of sex, some positions derive a fundamental equality and thereby the arbitrariness of different configurations of sexuality, whether as monogamous, polygamous, heterosexual, homosexual, or transsexual. Behind such positions stands a neo-Gnostic body-soul dualism, which fails to recognize the unity and holism of the human being (see I Cor 1:12–20). According to Christian conviction, the body, even in its sexuality, is a real symbol of the soul and the soul is the body's defining life-form. It is important to add that establishing the fact of differentiation in no way entails or justifies discrimination (see CCC 2357–59).

8. Proceeding from its overall personal approach, we may interpret Paul VI's encyclical concerning responsible parenthood,

Humanae Vitae (1968), in this holistic sense. Similarly, FC 29 and 31f.

9. Benedict XVI, encyclical *Caritas in Veritate* (2009), 1–9, 30, 33.

10. Concerning this, see the Pontifical Council for the Family's Charter of the Rights of the Family (1983) and the Pontifical Council, Justice and Peace's Compendium of the Church's Social Teaching (2004), 209–54.

11. See Mark 10:2–12; Luke 16:18; 1 Cor 7:10f. Concerning the provisions dealing with adultery, Matt 5:32 and 19:9, and concerning 1 Cor 7:15, see section 5 below and excursus 2.

12. Augustine, *On Marriage and Concupiscence*, 1:10, 11; *On Adulterous Marriages*; Sermon 392:2.

13. Chrysostom, *In genesim Sermo*, 6:2; 7:1.

14. John Paul II, encyclical *Redemptoris Missio* 51; FC 21, 49–64; CCC 1655–58; *Lumen Fidei*, 52f.

15. John Paul II, apostolic exhortation *Catechesi Tradendae* (1979), 68.

16. A problem, which can only be pointed to here, arises for confessionally mixed marriages and families, which cannot fully share together in the Eucharist.

17. Concerning Sunday, see John Paul II, apostolic exhortation *Dies Domini* (1998), 55–57. Concerning the spirituality of the *communio*: apostolic exhortation *Novo Millennio Ineunte* (2001), 43.

18. See Joseph Ratzinger, "Zur Frage der Unauflöslichkeit der Ehe: Bemerkungen zum dogmengeschichtlichen Befund und seiner gegenwärtigen Bedeutung," in *Ehe und Ehescheidung*, eds. Franz Heinrich and Volker Eid (Munich: Kösel Verlag, 1972), 35, 56. Cf. excursus 2 concerning the following.

19. See the Council of Trent: DH 1542 and 1672.

20. Council of Nicaea, canon 8; by converting to the Catholic Church, "so-called pure ones" are required as follows: "They must foster community both with those who live in a second marriage as well as with those who lapsed during persecution."

21. Benedict, *Rule*, 64:17–19. Said more generally, for Thomas prudence is the foundation, root, and guiding principle of every good life: *Summa Theologiae*, I/II, q. 57, a. 6; q. 58, a.4

22. Thomas Aquinas, *Summa Theologiae*, I/II, q. 64, a. 1f; *De Virt.*, a.13.

23. See Thomas Aquinas, *Summa Theologiae*, II/II, q. 1, a. 7.

24. See the excursus in the German edition of Thomas's works (Munich and Salzburg, 1950), volume 15:431–37.

CONCLUDING COMMENT ON THE DISCUSSION

FIRST I HAVE TO SAY THANK YOU. In particular, I thank the Holy Father for his friendly words and for his confidence in having entrusted me with this report. I thank everyone for their patience in having listened to me for so long. I have to say thanks both for the affirmative responses as well as for the more or less critical reactions. I would not like to nor can I go into all of the individual reactions, but I will limit myself to three points.

1. We agree that Jesus' words, according to which human beings cannot separate what God has joined together (Matt 19:6), must be the starting point and foundation of all our reflections. No one questions the indissolubility of a sacramental marriage that was contracted and consummated (*ratum* and *consumatum*).

We also indeed agree that one may not isolate the words of Jesus from the total context of his message about the kingdom of God and his message concerning the love and mercy of God. Rather, we agree that one must interpret his words in this context. Likewise, one must understand the doctrine of the indissolubility of marriage from the inner connection of the mysteries of faith (so says the First Vatican Council; see DH 3016) and within the hierarchy of the truths of faith (so says the Second Vatican Council in UR 11). One must, therefore, understand and actualize the words of Jesus and the teaching of the Church in connection with Jesus' message of God's infinite mercy for everyone who repents and desires his mercy. By doing this, we agree that mercy is no cheap grace. It does not dispense with personal conversion and, of course, it does not abolish the truth. Mercy is bound to the truth, but conversely the truth is also bound to mercy. Mercy is the hermeneutical principle for the interpretation of truth. It is necessary to do the truth in love (Eph 4:15).

There is an additional hermeneutical principle. According to the Catholic understanding, one must construe the words of Jesus in the context of the entire tradition of the Church. The tradition in our case is not at all so unilinear, as is often asserted. There are historical questions and diverse opinions from serious experts, which one cannot simply disregard. The Church has repeatedly sought to find a path beyond rigorism and laxity, that is, it has sought to do the truth in love.

2. The uniqueness of every person is a fundamental component of Christian anthropology. No human being is simply an instance of general human nature, and no human being can be judged only according to a general rule. Jesus never spoke of an "ism," neither individualism, consumerism, capitalism, relativism, nor pansexualism, and so on. In a parable, Jesus spoke of the Good Shepherd who leaves the

ninety-nine sheep in order to seek the one sheep that went astray, in order to put it on his shoulders when he finds it, and to return it to the herd. Jesus adds, "Just so, I tell you, there will be more joy in heaven over one sinner who repents than over ninety-nine righteous people who need no repentance" (Luke 15:1–7).

In other words: there are not *the* divorced and remarried; rather, there are divorced and remarried individuals who are in very different situations, which one must carefully distinguish. There also is not *the* objective situation, which poses an obstacle to admission to communion, but rather many very different objective situations. If, let's say, a woman was abandoned due to no fault of her own and, for the sake of her children, she needs a husband or a father, and she honestly endeavors to live a Christian life in the second, civilly contracted marriage and family, and she raises her children as Christians and is involved in her parish in exemplary fashion (which is very often the case), then this too belongs to the objective situation, which is essentially different from the situation that, unfortunately, very often occurs, when someone enters into a second, civil marriage, in a more or less religiously indifferent way, and also lives, more or less, unchurched.

Therefore, one may not proceed from a concept of the objective situation that has been reduced to one single point. Rather, we must seriously ask ourselves whether we really believe in the forgiveness of sins, which we indeed confess in the Creed, and whether we truly believe that someone who has made a mistake, regrets it, and cannot reverse it without incurring new guilt, but does everything that is possible for him- or herself, can obtain forgiveness from God, and whether we then can deny absolution to him or her? Would that be the stance of the Good Shepherd and the Good Samaritan?

For such particular cases, the Catholic tradition admittedly does not recognize, like the Orthodox churches, the principle of *oikonomia*, but it does know the similar principle of *epikeia*, the distinguishing of spirits, and equiprobabilism (St. Alphonsus Liguori). It recognizes the Thomistic understanding of the foundational cardinal virtue—prudence—which applies a general norm to the concrete situation (which, in Thomas Aquinas's sense, has nothing to do with situation ethics).

In short: in our current matter, there is no general solution for all cases. It is not a matter of *the* admission of *the* divorced and remarried. Rather, one must take seriously the uniqueness of every person and every situation and, case by case, carefully distinguish and decide. In that way, the path of conversion and penance, as the ancient church frequently recognized, is not the path of the great masses, but rather the path of particular Christians, who are truly serious about the sacraments.

3. Blessed John Henry Newman has written the famous essay, "On Consulting the Faithful in Matters of Faith." He has shown that, in the Arian crisis in the fourth and fifth centuries, it was not the bishops, but rather the faithful who preserved the faith of the Church. At the time, Newman was much criticized, but by saying what he did, he has become a forerunner of the Second Vatican Council, which has again clearly emphasized the teaching concerning the sense of faith, which is given to every Christian by virtue of baptism (LG 12, 35).

It is necessary to take seriously believers' sense of faith, precisely with regard to our current topic. We here in the Consistory are all celibates; most of the faithful, however, live out their belief in the gospel of the family in concrete families and sometimes in difficult situations. Therefore, we should listen to their witness and also listen to what pastoral coworkers and counselors in pastoral care to families have to say to us. And they do have something to say to us. The entire matter, therefore, cannot be decided simply by a commission to which only cardinals and bishops belong. That does not rule out that the last word will be given at the Synod, in agreement with the pope.

In this matter, there are great expectations in the Church. Beyond a doubt, we cannot fulfill all expectations. But it would cause a terrible disappointment if we would only repeat the answers that supposedly have always been given. As witnesses of hope, we may not allow ourselves to be led by a hermeneutic of fear. Some courage and above all biblical candor (*parrhesia*) are necessary. If we don't want that, then we should not hold a synod on this topic, because then the situation would be worse afterwards than before. We should at least open the door a crack for people's hope and expectations and at least give a sign that we, for our part, take seriously the hopes as well as the questions, anguish, and tears of so many serious Christians.

AFTERWORD:
WHAT CAN WE DO?

CONVERSATIONS OVER MANY YEARS with pastors, marriage and family counselors, and with affected married couples and families preceded the reflections that have been presented in the Consistory. Immediately after the lecture such conversations spontaneously erupted again. Above all, spiritual confrères wanted for the most part to know very quickly what they concretely should do or may do. These questions are understandable and justified. However, there are no simple recipes; nor can one bring about certain solutions in the Church with a sledgehammer, whether on one's own authority or by adopting a threatening posture. Many steps are necessary in order to arrive at a preferably unanimous solution.

The first step generally consists in once again becoming able to speak in matters of sexuality, marriage, and family, and finding a way out of the rigidity of resigned silence in light of the given situation. The mere question of what is permitted and what is forbidden doesn't help any further. Questions of marriage and family, under which the question of

the divorced and remarried is indeed only one question—
even though a pressing question—belong in the larger context of the question of how people can find happiness and
fulfillment in their lives. Dealing with the gift of sexuality,
given and entrusted to human beings by the Creator, in a
responsible and fulfilling way belongs essentially to this subject. Sexuality is supposed to lead out of the narrowness and
solitude of inward-looking individualism and lead to the You
of another human being and to the We of human community.
Isolating sexuality from such integral human relations and
reducing it to sex have not led to the much-vaunted libera-
tion, but rather to the banalization and commercialization
of sexuality. The death of erotic love and the senescence of
our Western society are the consequences. Marriage and
family are the last pocket of resistance against a coldly cal-
culating and all-consuming economization and mechaniza-
tion of life. We have every reason to support the cause of
marriage and family life to the best of our abilities and, above
all, to accompany and encourage young people on this path.

A second step within the Church consists in a renewed
pastoral spirituality that takes leave of a narrow, legalistic
view and an unchristian rigorism that places on people intol-
erable burdens that we clerics ourselves do not want to bear
and also could not bear (see Matt 23:4). With their principle
of *oikonomia*, the Eastern churches have developed a way
beyond rigorism and laxity, from which we can learn ecu-
menically. In the West, we know *epikeia*, justice in individual
cases, which is the higher righteousness, according to
Thomas Aquinas. *Oikonomia* is not primarily a matter of a
canonical principle, but rather a spiritual and pastoral basic
attitude that applies the gospel like a good *paterfamilias*,

understood as *oikonomos*, in conformity to the model of the divine economy of salvation. In his economy of salvation, God has gone many steps with his people and has gone a long way with the Church in the Holy Spirit. In a similar way, the Church is supposed to accompany people when they make their incremental approach to life's goal and, in the process, the Church should be aware that we too, as pastors, are also underway and often enough do wrong and must begin anew. And, because of the never-ending mercy of God, we may repeatedly begin again.

Oikonomia is not a cheap path or an expedient escape. It takes seriously that, as Martin Luther formulated it correctly in the first of his Ninety-Five Theses in 1517, the entire Christian life is one of penance, that is, a life of repeatedly new rethinking and reorientation (*metanoia*). That we have often forgotten this and have culpably neglected the sacrament of penance as the sacrament of mercy is one of the deepest wounds of contemporary Christianity. The way of penance (*via paenitentialis*) is, therefore, not only something for the divorced and remarried, but also for all Christians. Only if we begin anew in pastoral care in this deep and comprehensive way will we also make progress, one step at a time, in the concrete issues that are pending.

The third step involves an institutional implementation of such anthropological and spiritual reflections. The sacrament of marriage as well as the sacrament of the Eucharist is not only a private, individual affair; they have a communitarian and public character and thus a juridical aspect. The church marriage ceremony is supposed to be shared by the entire community of the church—concretely, the parish—while the civil marriage ceremony stands under the protection of the constitution and the legal system of the state. Viewed in this larger context, canonical procedures in marriage questions are in need of a spiritual and pastoral reorientation. Nowadays there already exists a far-reaching consensus that one-sidedly administrative and legalistic procedures, according to the principle of tutiorism,[1] cannot do justice to the health and well-being of people and their concrete, often very complex life situations. That is not a plea for a more lax handling and expansion of annulments, but it is indeed a plea for a simplification and acceleration of these procedures and, above all, for their being embedded in pastoral and spiritual conversations and counseling, in the spirit of the Good Shepherd and the Good Samaritan.

Above all, a fourth step is being hotly debated concerning situations in which an annulment of the first marriage is not possible or, as in not a few cases, is not desired because it would be dishonest. The Church should encourage, accompany, and, in every respect, support those who, after a civil divorce, go the difficult path of being alone. New forms of domestic churches can be a great help here and can provide them with a new spiritual home. The path of permitting divorced people, who are civilly remarried, to receive the sacrament of penance and the Eucharist in concrete situations, after a period of reorientation, is being taken in some individual cases with the acquiescence or silent approval of the bishop. This discrepancy between the official regulations and the silent praxis on the ground is not a good situation. Even when casuistry is not possible or is not desirable, binding criteria should exist and be publicly identified. I have attempted that in my lecture. This attempt can, of course, be improved. Nevertheless, the hope of very many people is justified that the forthcoming Synod, guided by God's Spirit and after consideration of all points of view, can point out a good path that all can endorse.[2]

NOTES

1. Translator's note: tutiorism is an ethical position that holds that, in cases when moral certitude is absent, the "safer" or more rigorous course of moral action should be taken.

2. An aid of great spiritual and pastoral wisdom, in the line of St. Alphonsus Liguori, the patron saint of moral theology, is the readable small book from Bernhard Häring: *No Way Out? Pastoral Care of the Divorced and Remarried* (Middlegreen, England: St. Paul Publications, 1990).